Language Development for Maths

Activities for Home

Marion Nash and Jackie Lowe

 David Fulton Publishers

David Fulton Publishers Ltd
The Chiswick Centre, 414 Chiswick High Road, London W4 5TF

David Fulton Publishers is a division of Granada Learning, part of ITV plc.

www.fultonpublishers.co.uk

First published in Great Britain by David Fulton Publishers 2004

10 9 8 7 6 5 4 3 2 1

British Library Cataloguing in Publication Data
A catalogue record for this book is available from the British Library.

ISBN 1–84312–172–7

Typeset by FiSH Books, London
Printed and bound in Great Britain

Contents

To both our families who have been so supportive,
thank you to each and every one of you.

Background

This book has been written to accompany *Language Development for Maths: Circle Time Sessions to Improve Language Skills* (see page 85 for details). It is one of a series of six books which support the Spirals programme of language development. This programme has been trialled in a number of schools and is proving highly successful in improving children's language skills, confidence and self-esteem.

Parents often express a wish to help their children with activities at home which are effective but also achievable in a busy lifestyle. These simple, play-based activities will help busy parents, carers and support workers to focus on the language that is used at home to aid the development of their children's learning in maths.

We have taken one key idea from each weekly Spirals session and built up a bank of learning experiences. These activity sheets can be photocopied and given to parents and carers to empower them to work in collaboration with their children's setting. The handbook can also stand alone in providing ideas for parents, teachers and speech and language therapists.

Jackie Lowe and Marion Nash

Acknowledgements

The publication of this book has been made possible by the enthusiasm, foresight and support of those people working in the Plymouth Teaching Primary Care Trust and the Plymouth Education Authority. We have been supported and encouraged by the managers and those who direct these services.

We must also acknowledge and thank those parents and professionals who worked with us, in developing the Spirals approach to the language of maths, within the Plymouth area.

Using the handbook

The ideas in this book are linked directly to the 36 sessions in the book *Language Development for Maths: Circle Time Sessions to Improve Language Skills*, which underpins the Spirals course (see p. 85).

Each page is designed to be used as a stand-alone handout to develop one key idea in a simple and user-friendly way. Parents and carers can use the ideas as play activities with their children at home.

The illustrations may also be given to act as a prompt for parents whose literacy skills are weak, or for whom English is an additional language. Coloured in and pinned to a wall at home, they also act as a visual reminder of simple games that can continue to be fun for all members of the family.

The aim is that one sheet will be given out <u>after</u> each session to reinforce concepts which have been introduced in that session. Active use of these sheets at home will further accelerate the children's learning and understanding, and encourage parents' involvement in establishing a strong bedrock for learning. Using these sheets will empower parents to work in collaboration with their child's setting and give them confidence that they are 'doing the right thing'.

The grid on each page is for the parent to indicate how the activity went – did it go very well, with the child enjoying it and showing by the end that he or she had understood the word and concept? The empty boxes are for the parent to tick and/or date each time they try the activity. If the sheets are handed in after use, this device can help the teacher to understand how much support is being offered at home; it can also act as a motivator for parents and carers.

Date	☺ Comment

Date	☺ Comment
4/5/04	Jason likes this
5/5/04	game. His sister
7/5/04	joined in. ☺

The worksheets in this book may also be used independently where necessary, to give support in particular areas of language development. The record sheets at the end of the book can be used by parents and/or teachers to keep track of activities used.

The number songs and rhymes are also provided at the back of the book as a resource for parents and carers.

Ideas for Home

First and last

Ideas for Home

Play the first and last game

Session 1: Understanding and using the words <u>first</u> and <u>last</u>

Date:............

Take some of your child's toys and line them up on the floor or table. If the toys have faces, put them all looking the same way. Pick up the first toy in the line and say, 'This toy is the first.' Then pick up the last toy in the line and say, 'This . . . is the last.'

Put them back in the same places.

Encourage your child to show you which is first and which is last.

Play this activity as much as you can during the week with the same toys or different ones. Encourage your child to say, e.g. 'Elephant first,' 'The teddy's last.'

There are lots of different ways we use the words first and last, e.g. 'I'll do this first' and 'You go first.' Think and talk about the number of times and different ways we use these words.

Date	☺ Comment

Same

Ideas for Home

Find things that are the same

Session 2: Understanding and using the word <u>same</u>

Date:............

Collect some objects or toys from around your home that match or look the same, e.g. 2 teaspoons, 2 pens, 2 plates, 2 combs.

Put them in a box or bag.

Take one out and say, 'Here's a comb/pen,' and put it in front of your child. Then find one the same in the box/bag, bring it out and say, 'Oh, here's another one... they are the same.'

Then keep one of all the objects and give your child the others in the bag or box.

Pick up one of your objects and say to your child, 'Find one the same.'

If they find this difficult, reduce the items to three and then see if they can find one the same. If they get stuck, show them which is the same and put it in front of them.

During the week point out things that are the same and say, 'These are the same' – things such as socks, gloves and shoes. Encourage your child to say the word 'same'.

Date	☺ Comment

Circle

Ideas for Home

Play the shape hunt game

Session 3: Learning to identify circles and say 'circle'

Date:............

Say to your child, 'We are going on a shape hunt.'

Walk around the house holding your child's hand and point out all the circles you can see, e.g. the front of the washing machine, knob handles, jam jar lids.

Run your finger around the shape and say, 'This is a circle.'

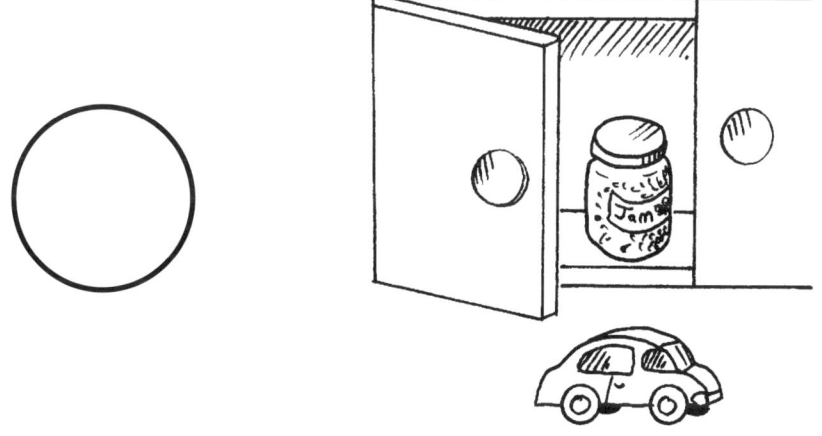

Look at things from different angles to find different shapes. Try to find as many circles as you can.

At another time ask your child if he/she can point out some circles to you. Encourage your child to say 'circle', 'big circle', 'little circle'.

Look out for circles during the week, inside and outside the house.

Date	☺ Comment

Square, side, corner

Ideas for Home

Continue the shape hunt game

Session 4: Identifying squares and using the words <u>square</u>, <u>side</u> and <u>corner</u>

Date:............

Walk around the house holding your child's hand and point out all the square shapes you can see. Look at the television, cards, bathroom tiles. Run your finger around the shape and encourage your child to do the same.

Say as you run your finger down the side, 'This is a side.' Then touch the corner and say, 'This is a corner.' Then say, 'This is a square shape.'

During the week look out for square shapes, inside and outside the house. Encourage your child to remember the words 'square', 'side' and 'corner'.

Date	☺ Comment

Triangle

Ideas for Home

Play another shape game

Session 5: Talking about triangles

Date:...........

Take a piece of square sliced bread and look at the shape of it with your child.

Talk about it being a square shape and it having sides and corners. Cut the bread in half to make a triangle shape. Say to your child, 'Look what shape I am going to make now. It's a triangle. It has three corners and three sides.' Encourage your child to count the corners and the sides.

Explore your house to see if you can find any other triangle shapes. Praise your child if he/she can see any.

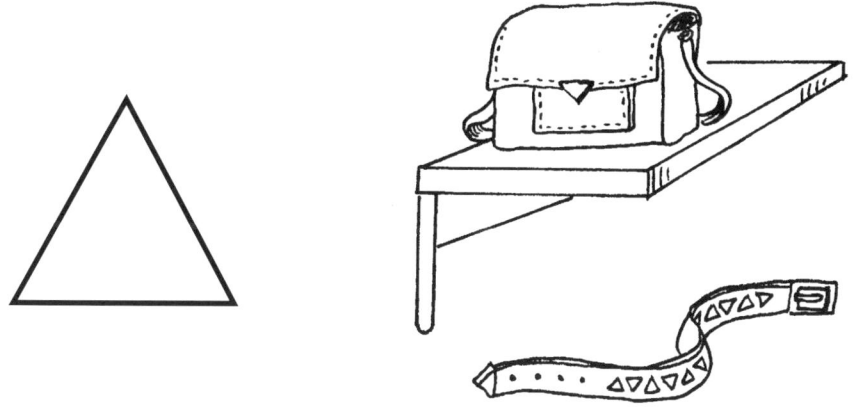

Take your child to a food shop in the week to see if you can pick out some triangle shapes, e.g. cheese or chocolate triangles.

Date	☺ Comment

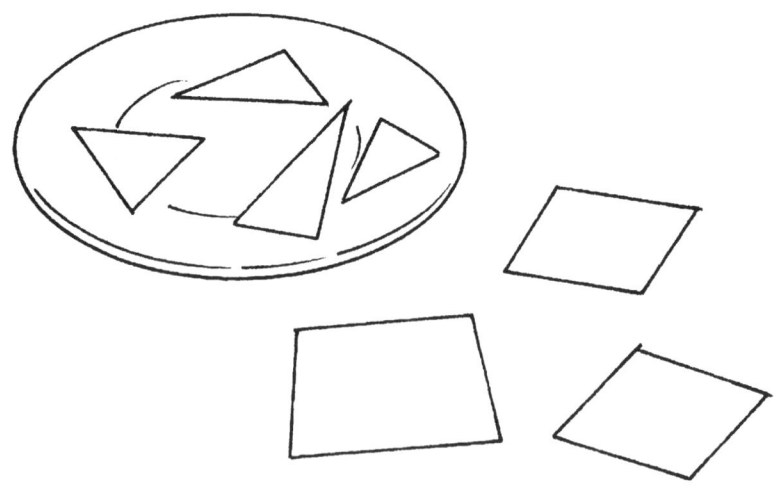

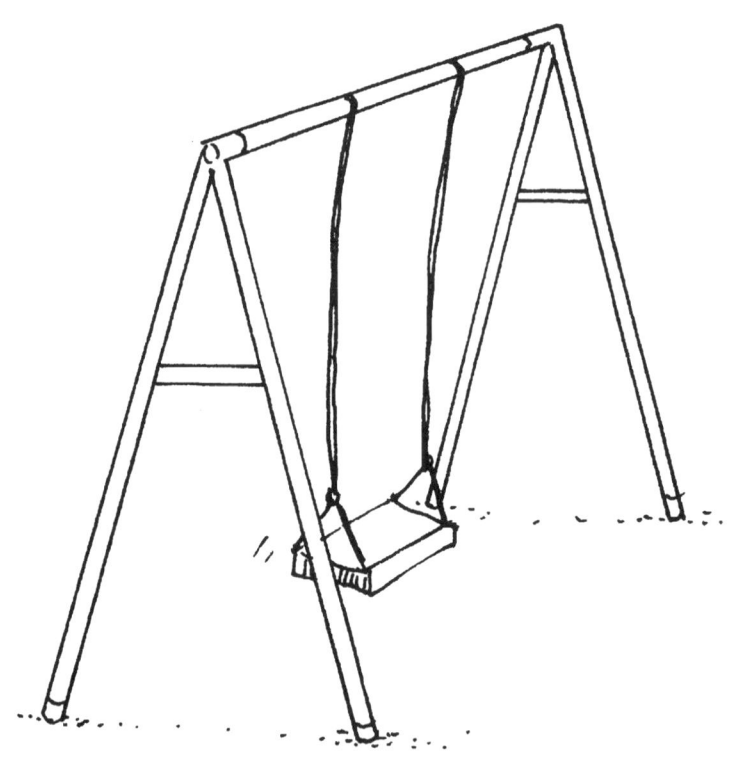

Triangle, square

Ideas for Home

Play the triangle game

Session 6: Using the words <u>triangle</u> and <u>square</u>

Date:...........

Look at a triangle cut from paper or card, or a plastic shape, and talk about how it has three sides and three corners. (There are shapes to cut out at the back of this book.)

Now look at a square and run a finger along its four sides. Count its four corners. Show your child that if you fold or cut the square in half, corner to corner, you can make two triangles.

Collect together a mix of squares and triangles and ask your child to sort them out: 'Put all the triangles on the plate and all the squares on the table.'

Look around outside, in the park or on the way to the shops or school, for examples of square and triangular shapes.

Date	☺ Comment

Two

Ideas for Home

Play the number 2 game

Session 7: Connecting the word and number 2

Date:............

Choose two things that your child likes to eat, e.g.
2 biscuits, 2 Smarties, or 2 crisps.

Lay them on a table in front of your child and point to each
item and say, 'There are one...two biscuits.'

Then on a piece of paper write the number 2. Point out the
number, encourage your child to trace the 2 shape with
his/her finger and say, 'That is number two.'

Date	☺ Comment

Heavy and light

Ideas for Home

Play the heavy and light game

Session 8: Understanding and using the words <u>heavy</u> and <u>light</u>

Date:...........

Find two carrier bags and fill one with lots of objects to make it heavy (food tins would be good). Put one thing in the other.

Ask your child to pick the first bag up and as they are trying to do it say, 'It's heavy.'

Then ask your child to pick up the other one. Say, 'This one is light.'

Ask your child to show you the heavy bag and praise him/her if they get it right.

Ask him/her which is light.

Talk about heavy and light things as much as you can in the week.

Make a collection of light things (paper, cotton wool) and heavy things (tins, books) to help your child learn these words.

Date	☺ Comment

Three

Ideas for Home

Play the clapping game

Session 9: Counting to three

Date:...........

Sit with your child and say, 'We are going to play a clapping game. Listen carefully.'

Make one clap and say 'one'. Ask your child to do the same. Then clap twice and say 'two'. Say, 'You do the same.'

Then clap three times and say 'three'. Say, 'You do the same.'

Encourage your child to do one clap, then two claps, then three claps and say 'one', 'two', 'three', corresponding to the claps they do.

During the week see if your child can make claps of the right number, such as, 'Give me three claps,' 'Give me two claps.'

Move on to five if your child can manage this.

Date	☺ Comment

Five

Ideas for Home

More clapping games

Session 10: Counting to five

Date:............

Say to your child, 'I want you to tell me how many claps I'm doing, listen carefully and count.' Then clap twice and see if your child can say 'two'. If he/she can't, encourage them to clap with you and count the claps together. 'One, two...'

Build up the guessing game until he/she can count to five.

If this goes well, do the same games with tapping.

Practise counting to five with fingers and toes.

Date	☺ Comment

Long and short

Ideas for Home

Play the long and short game

Session 11: Understanding and using the words <u>long</u> and <u>short</u>

Date:............

Take a piece of paper and a pen and draw a very long line.
Say to your child, 'This is a long line.' Then draw a short line.
As you are doing it say, 'This is a short line.'

Encourage your child to draw a long line and say 'long'. Then say,
'Can you draw me a short line?' Give your child lots of praise.
Make some more lines together. Talk about the lines with your
child: 'Which ones are short?', 'Which ones are long?'

Talk about long and short things in the week.
Look out among your family and friends for people who have long
or short hair.

Think about the different ways we use the word 'long', e.g. 'long
time', 'short time'.

Date	☺ Comment

Shapes

Ideas for Home

Play more shape games

Session 12: Making circles, squares, triangles, etc.

Date:............

Get three large pieces of paper. Say to your child, 'We are going to make some shapes out of the paper.' Ask your child, 'Shall I make a circle or a triangle?' Whichever your child chooses, draw that shape on the paper and then cut it out.

Draw a square, a circle and a triangle and cut each of them out.

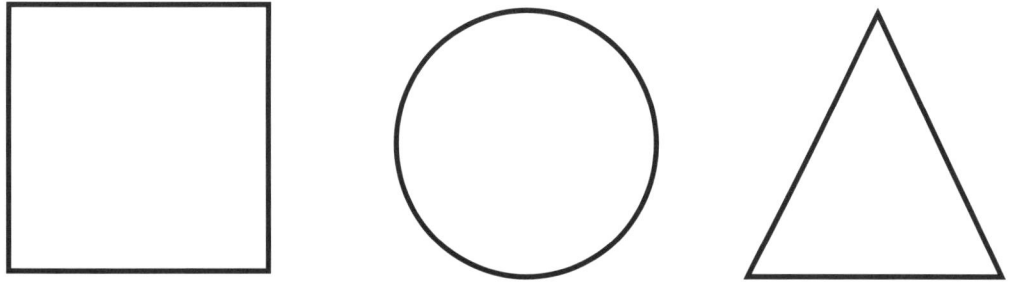

Hold up the circle and say, 'This has one edge; it goes all the way round, without any corners.'

Give your child the triangle and ask, 'Can you show me the corners?'

Give him/her the square and ask, 'How many corners has the square got?'

Make some more circle, triangle and square shapes. Lay them out on the floor. Pick out one and ask, 'Can you find one the same?'

With your child put all the circles together, all the squares together and all the triangles together and talk about what they are like or describe them.

Then lay them out in lines and talk about which one is first and which one is last in the line.

Date	😊 Comment

Heaviest

Ideas for Home

Play the heaviest bag game

Session 13: Understanding and using the word <u>heaviest</u>

Date:...........

Find three carrier bags from the supermarket and put in a few items from the cupboard: tins, cereal packets, etc. (Make sure that one bag is heavier than the other two.)

Pick up one and say to your child, 'This one is heavy.' Pick up another bag and say, 'This one is heavy too.' Pick up another and say, 'This one is heavy as well.'

Ponder on them and ask your child, 'Which one is the **heaviest** bag?'

Pick out the heaviest and then say, 'This is the heaviest bag.' Say to your child, 'Show me the heaviest bag.'

Talk about heavy things in the week – at the shops, in the home. Try to decide with your child which is the heaviest. Encourage your child to use the word 'heaviest'.

Date	☺ Comment

Lightest

Ideas for Home

Play the lightest bag game

Session 14: Understanding and using the word <u>lightest</u>

Date:...........

Find three carrier bags and put some light things in them, e.g. folded paper, a cereal box, an empty box, a feather or sponge. (Make sure that one bag is lighter than the other two.)

Lift up one of the bags and say, 'This one is light.' Lift up another bag and say, 'This one is light too.'

Ask your child, 'Which one is **lightest**?' Say, 'This one is the lightest.'

Make a collection of light things on a tray, e.g. cotton wool, leaf, sponge, tissue paper.

Talk with your child about which is the lightest. Encourage your child to say, 'This is the lightest.'

Date	☺ Comment

Longest

Ideas for Home

Play find the longest string

Session 15: Understanding and using the word <u>longest</u>

Date:...........

Find three pieces of string, wool or ribbon. Make them different lengths – but all quite long.

Sit with your child on the floor and put out the strings, taking it in turns. Say, when it is your turn, 'This one is long.'
Lay the strings on the floor beside you.
Say, 'This one is long, this one is long. Which one is the **longest**?'
Pause, 'Hmm...this one is the longest, can you see?'

Ask your child to show you the longest string and say, 'This is the longest string.'

In the week talk about long and longest. Talk about all the people you know with long hair. 'Who has the longest hair?'

Date	☺ Comment

Shortest

Ideas for Home

Play find the shortest string

Session 16: Understanding and using the word <u>shortest</u>

Date:............

Find five pieces of string, wool or ribbon. Make them different short lengths.

Lay the strings on the floor beside you.
When you have taken the strings out, look at them and say, 'This one is short, this one is quite short as well. Which one is the **shortest**?' Pause, 'Hmm...this one is the shortest, can you see?'

Ask your child to show you the shortest string and say, 'This is the shortest string.'

In the week talk about long and short things. Talk about which is the shortest. Talk about all the people you know with short hair. 'Who has the shortest hair?'

When your child feels confident, introduce the long strings from the last session and take it in turns to pull all of the strings out of a bag, saying, 'I have a long string.' Take a turn with your child to name the long and short strings and the longest and shortest strings.

Date	☺ Comment

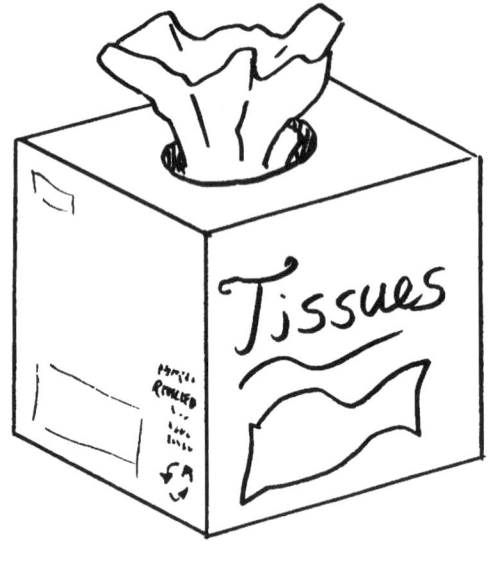

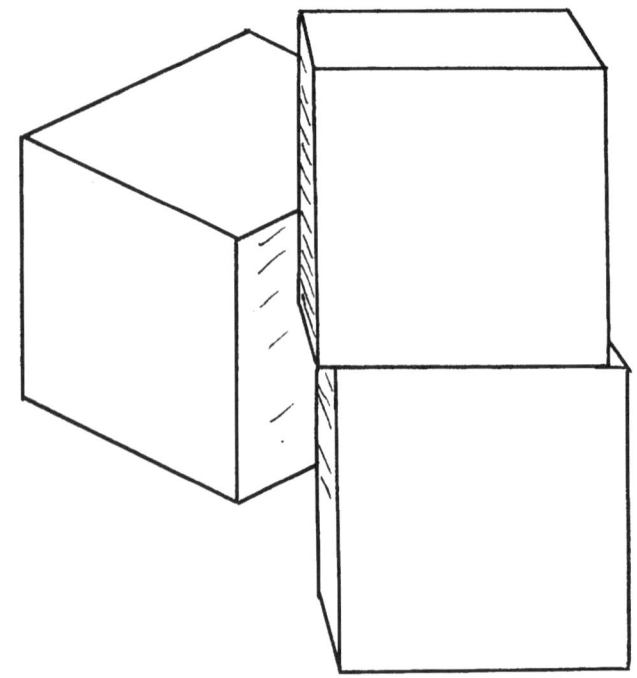

Cubes

Ideas for Home

Explore the idea of a cube

Session 17: Introducing the word <u>cube</u> and what it means

Date:............

Find a cube in your house. This could be a toy brick, with six equal faces, an Oxo cube, a sugar cube, or a box (some tissue boxes are cubes). You will also need a pen or some stickers.

Put the cube in front of your child and say, 'This is a cube; it has six square faces.' Point to the faces with your child, and encourage your child to point to each one. You could mark each of the six faces with a sticker or cross.

Look around the house for other cubes. Use the word cube as much as you can in the week.

Date	☺ Comment

Semicircle

Ideas for Home

Make a semicircle

Session 18: Showing what a semicircle is and using the word

Date:............

You will need two or three Jaffa Cakes and a knife.

Choose a round Jaffa Cake (easier than a biscuit, because it won't crack when you cut it). Show your child and say, 'Can you remember what shape this cake is?' Praise him if he says 'circle'. If not, help him.

Say, 'Now I'm going to cut it in half and make half a circle; we call that a **semicircle**.' Cut the cake in half. Show your child what you have made; encourage your child to look at it and to feel the curved edge and the straight edge.

Give your child another Jaffa Cake and encourage them to make another semicircle.

Look around the house with your child, seeing if you can find anything else that is a semicircle, and keep using the word.

Date	☺ Comment

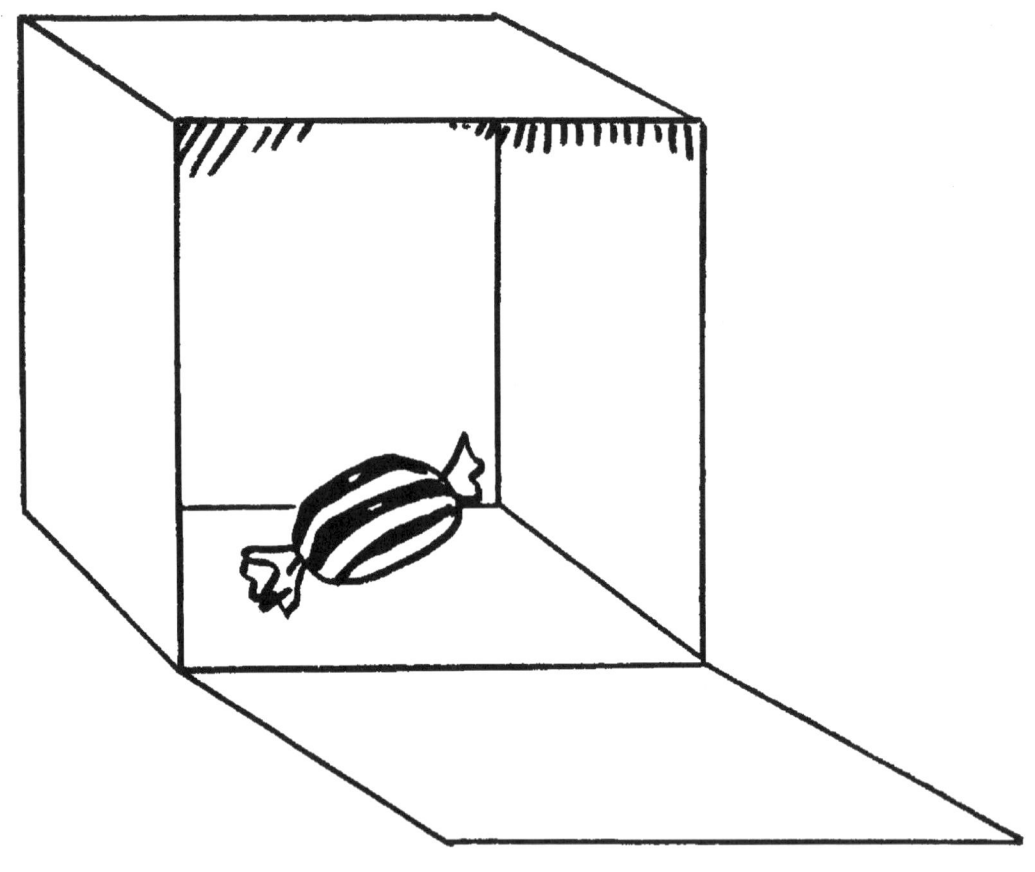

Make a cube

Ideas for Home

Make a cube

Session 19: Making a cube and using the word

Date:...........

You will need the template enclosed for the squares, some scissors and a sweet or small toy.

Find some card and cut it into six squares. Use the template enclosed.

Say to your child, 'I have some squares here.' Spend some time looking at the corners, edges and faces.

'Now we are going to make these into a cube.' Use Sellotape to tape the pieces of card together to make a cube.

Say, 'This is a cube.'

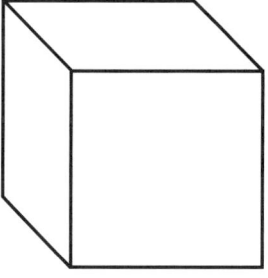

Keep one square fixed by one edge only so that something can be hidden inside the cube. Find something little and put it inside the cube.

Each day put something else in the cube. Encourage your child to say what is in the cube, e.g. 'The Smartie's in the cube.'

Date	☺ Comment

One more, one less

Ideas for Home

Play the apples in the box game

Session 20: Introducing the words <u>one more</u>, <u>one less</u>, <u>too many</u> and <u>left over</u>

Date:...........

You will need a plastic container with a lid and enough apples to fill it and have one or two left over.

Say, 'How many apples will fit into the box?'
Count the apples as you put them in the box.
Talk about filling the box. Play a game with your child using questions such as, 'Can you fit **one more** in?', 'Shall we try and put the lid on?', 'Can we put one more in?'
Overfill the box and say, 'One **too many**. We need **one less**.'
When the box is full and the lid is on, talk about how many apples are **left over**.

Over the week repeat this activity with different fruit or vegetables and different-sized boxes.
Encourage your child to use the words 'one more' and 'too many', and check how many are 'left over'.

Date	☺ Comment

Cylinder

Ideas for Home

Make a cylinder

Session 21: Using the word <u>cylinder</u>

Date:............

Collect a tube left over from a kitchen roll, toilet roll, or clingfilm roll. You will need a piece of paper, some Sellotape, a pencil and scissors.
Show the tube to your child and say, 'This is a **tube**.'

Let your child hold the tube, look through it and hold it. Talk about the end being a circle.

Turn the tube on its end and stand it on a piece of paper; draw around it to make a circle template the same size as the end. Cut out two of these paper circles with your child and Sellotape one of them on one end of the tube. Say to your child, 'We are making a **cylinder**.'

Put something little in the cylinder before you Sellotape the second end up; for example, a Smartie. Say to your child, 'Where's the Smartie gone? It's in the cylinder.' Shake the cylinder that you have made, saying, 'It's in the cylinder.'
Ask your child during the week, 'Where's the Smartie?'

Try to look for tubes and cylinders during the week.

Date	☺ Comment

Ideas for Home

Play the shapes game

Session 22: Using the words <u>square</u>, <u>triangle</u>, <u>circle</u>, <u>semicircle</u>, <u>different</u>, <u>same</u>, <u>biggest</u> and <u>smallest</u>

Date:............

You will need some paper, a pencil and scissors.

Draw some circles, squares, triangles and semicircles. Make the triangles different shapes. Make the squares, circles and semicircles different sizes.

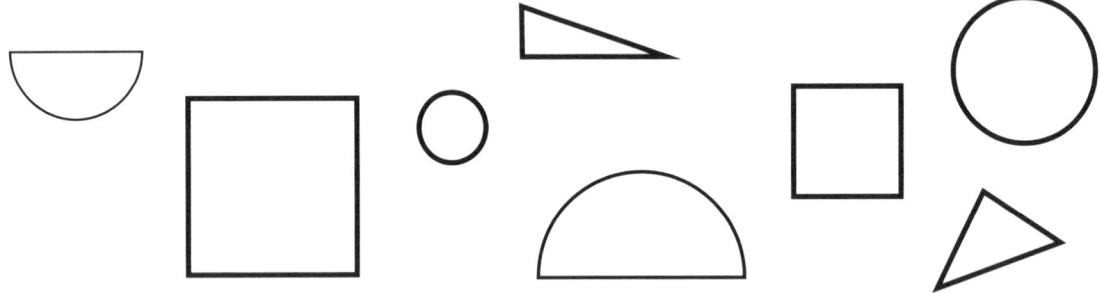

Talk to your child about the big and small or little circles, semicircles, triangles and squares.
Talk about the shape that is the **biggest** and the **smallest**.
Cut out all the shapes, talking about them as you do so, e.g. 'This is a little circle.' Encourage your child to say which ones they want you to cut around next.

Put the shapes into piles and talk about **same** and **different**.

Play games during the week with your child, getting him/her to ask for

- the biggest circle
- the smallest triangle
- all the triangles
- one more circle.

Date	☺ Comment

Ideas for Home

Play hiding the shapes

Session 23: Using the words <u>square</u>, <u>triangle</u>, <u>circle</u> and <u>semicircle</u>, and position words such as <u>under</u>, <u>behind</u> and <u>next to</u>

Date:...........

You will need the shapes you made for the last session.

Spread all the shapes out in front of your child. Explain to your child that you want him/her to tell you where to hide the shape, e.g. 'Put a square under the sofa.'

'Put a semicircle behind the telly.'

You can take it in turns choosing where to put the shapes.

Date	😊 Comment

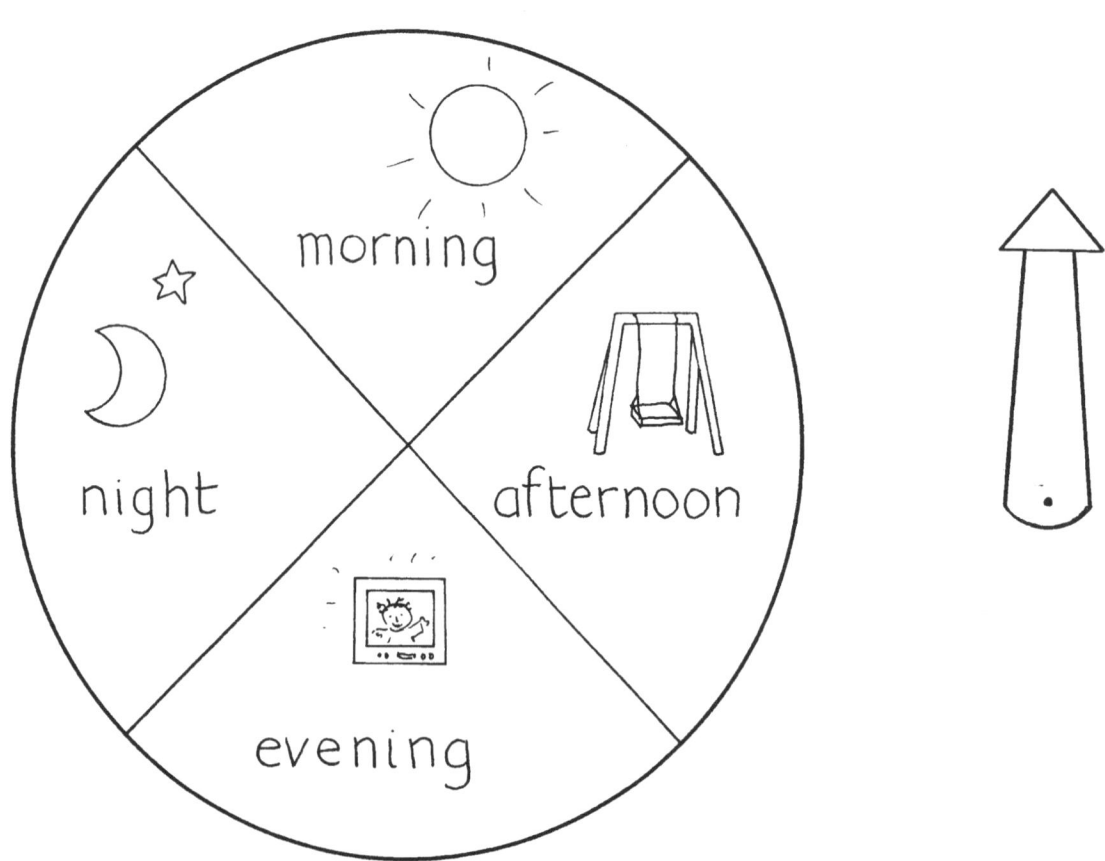

Time

Ideas for Home

Make a time wheel

Session 24: Talking about the <u>time</u>

Date:............

Make a time wheel with your child, using the template provided.

- In the morning point the arrow to the morning and say to your child, 'This is the **morning**.'
- Around midday bring the arrow round to the afternoon and say to your child, 'All that time has passed. The morning is over now; it's the **afternoon**.'
- At teatime bring the arrow round again and say to your child, 'Now it is the **evening**.'
- When your child is about to go to bed, bring the arrow to night and say to your child, 'Now it is **night time**.'
- Say to your child, 'This makes **one whole day**.'

Repeat this time wheel for at least two days. During the week try to bring your child's attention to the time wheel when you are in the house. So in the morning you can set the arrow to the morning; when your child comes home from school move the arrow to the afternoon or evening. Help your child to realise that time has passed, emphasising the words 'morning', 'afternoon', 'evening' and 'night time'.

Date	☺ Comment

Ideas for Home

Play the time game

Session 25: Using the words morning, afternoon, evening and night

                                        Date:............

Talk about what you do in the **morning**: get up, eat breakfast, play, go to nursery/school, etc.
Draw pictures or cut out the ones given here, and stick them on your time wheel.

Talk about what you do in the **afternoon**: eat lunch, go shopping, visit friends/Granny, etc., play in the park.
Cut these out and stick them on your time wheel.

Talk about what you do in the **evening**: eat tea, watch telly, have a bath, play games.
Draw pictures or cut out the ones given. Stick them on the evening part of the time wheel.

Talk about what we do at **night**. Draw a picture of a bed or use the picture enclosed. Stick the picture on night.

Say to your child, 'This makes up **one whole day**.'

Talk to your child as much as you can during the week about the morning, afternoon and evening, and repeat that this makes up one day.

Date	☺ Comment

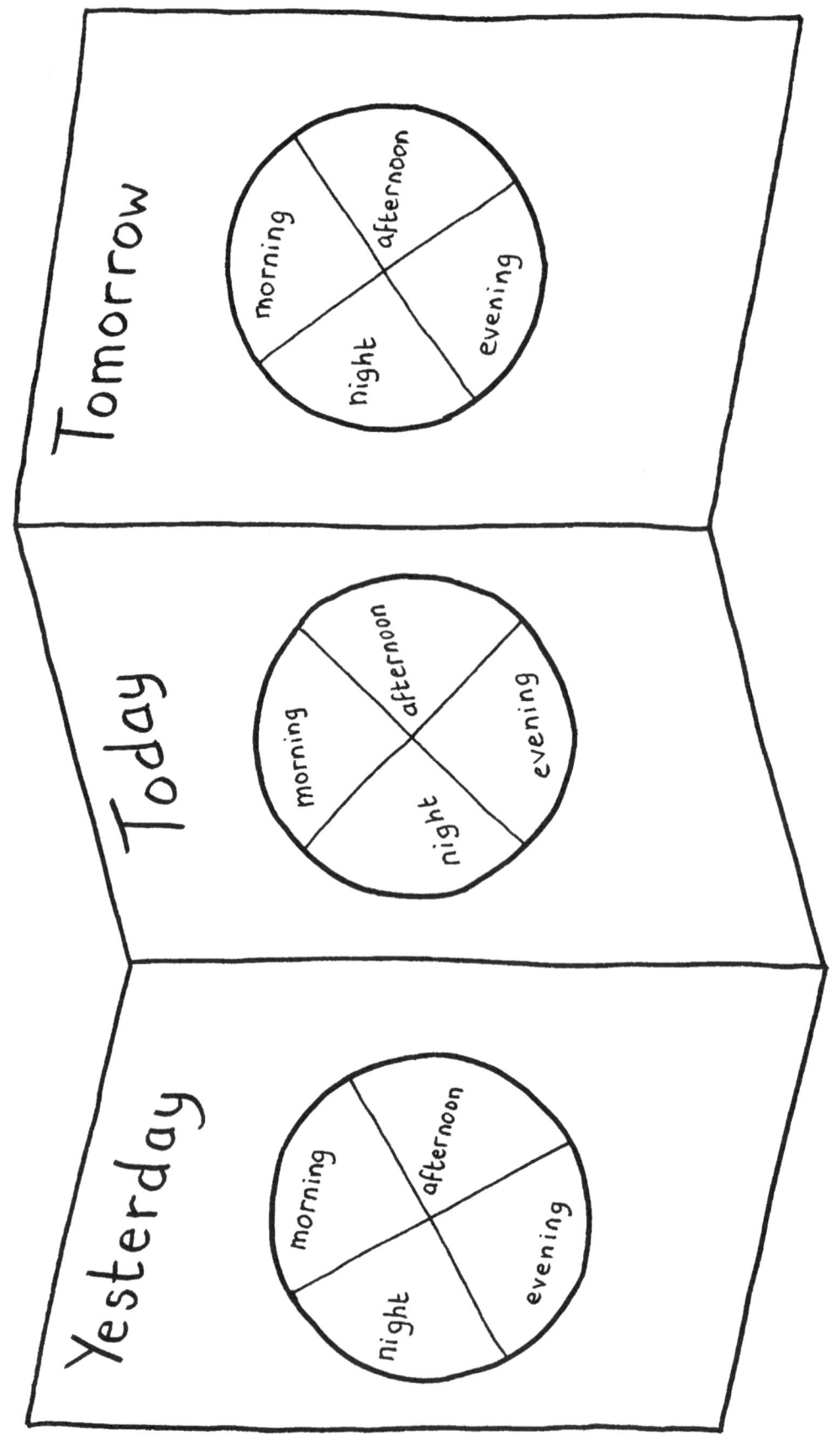

Ideas for Home

Play more talking time games

Session 26: Introducing the time words <u>today</u>, <u>tomorrow</u> and <u>yesterday</u>

Date:............

You will need the time wheel that you have made before.

Continue using the arrow in your time wheel to help your child understand a day.

Say to your child, 'This day is called **today**. What we do on the time wheel from breakfast to the next morning is today.' Run your finger around the time wheel and encourage your child to do the same.

'What we did on the time wheel in the last day is called **yesterday**.'

'What we are going to do when we wake up in the morning is **tomorrow**.'

Talk to your child as much as you can in the week about today, what you did and where you went yesterday, and what you will do tomorrow.

Date	☺ Comment

2+1=3

Add

Ideas for Home

Play the adding game

Session 27: Introducing the word <u>add</u>

Date:............

You will need some biscuits or sweets.

Lay out two biscuits. Ask, 'How many biscuits have I got?' If your child can count them on his/her own let him do that and give him lots of praise. If not, help him: 'One, two.'

Then say, 'I'm going to **add** one more.' Bring another biscuit out. Ask, 'How many have I got now?' If your child can count on his own, let him do this and give him lots of praise: 'That's right, well done.' If he can't, say, 'I have added one more; now I have three.'
Bring out the ✚ sign. Say this means **add**.

Talk to your child as much as you can in the week about adding: 'I am adding sugar to Daddy's tea.'
'Let's add something else to the shopping trolley,' etc.
'Here are two apples; let's add one more – how many are there now? That's right, three.'

Date	☺ Comment

Take away

Ideas for Home

Play the taking away game

Session 28: Introducing the words <u>take away</u>

Date:............

Hold up one hand and

- Ask your child, 'How many fingers am I holding up?' Give your child a chance to count them. Say, 'I'm going to **take one away**.' Put your hand behind your back and fold back one of your fingers so that only four are standing up.
- Ask your child, 'How many fingers can you see?' Encourage your child to count them and then say, 'I'm going to **take one away**.' Put your hand behind your back again and fold down two fingers.
- Ask your child, 'How many fingers can you see now?' Encourage your child to count them and then say, 'I'm going to **take one away**.' Put your hand behind your back again and fold down three fingers.
- Ask your child, 'How many fingers can you see now?' Encourage your child to count them and then say, 'I'm going to **take one away**.' Put your hand behind your back again and fold down four fingers.
- Ask your child, ' How many fingers can you see now?' Encourage your child to count them and then say, 'I'm going to **take one away**.' Put your hand behind your back again and fold down five fingers.
- Ask, 'How many fingers can you see?' If they say 'none' that is fine but if not help them by saying, 'They have all gone.'

Play this take away game as much as you can in the week.
You can play with objects under a cloth instead of fingers.

Date	☺ Comment

55

Ideas for Home

Play the forwards and backwards game

Session 29: Introducing the words <u>forwards</u> and <u>backwards</u>

Date:............

Stand holding hands with your child in the garden or in a room at home.

Still holding hands say, 'We are going to play a walking game. You do as I do.' Walk forwards with your child and say, 'We are walking **forwards**.'
Then still holding hands walk backwards and say, 'We are walking **backwards**.'

Play this game several times until your child can anticipate which way you are going when you say 'backwards' or 'forwards'.
See if your child can walk backwards or forwards on their own.

Use toy figures or toy cars to practise understanding and using the words 'forwards' and 'backwards'.

Date	☺ Comment

Ideas for Home

More forwards and backwards games

Session 30: Using the words <u>forwards</u> and <u>backwards</u>

Date:...........

Say to your child, 'We are going to play a new forwards and backwards game. You tell me to walk forwards or backwards.'

Encourage your child to say, 'Mum walk forwards.' Then you walk forwards. Then say, 'What next?' Encourage them to say, 'Walk backwards.'

Introduce different numbers of steps: 'Walk forwards two steps. Walk backwards one step,' etc.

Keep on playing this game until your child gets quicker at using the words.

During the week involve other members of the family: Granny, Daddy, brothers, etc.

Date	☺ Comment

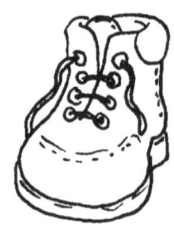

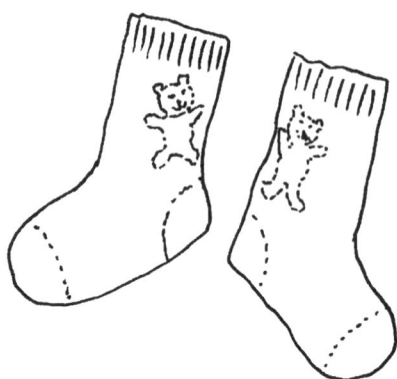
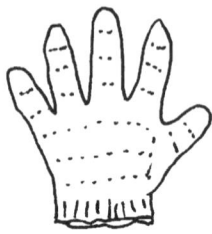

Twos

Ideas for Home

Play the counting in twos game

Session 31: Counting in twos

Date:............

Line up everyone's shoes, socks or gloves (in pairs). Or use small sweets.

Instead of counting them one by one, group them in twos and count them in front of your child: '2, 4, 6, 8, 10, 12.' Then say it again. Repeat this activity five times and then put the items away or eat them.

In the week count in twos each day so that your child hears the pattern. See if he can join in but don't force him.

2, 4, 6

2, 4, 6, 8

2, 4, 6, 8, 10

Date	☺ Comment

1

2

Numbers

Ideas for Home

Play drawing numbers

Session 32: Introducing number shapes

Date:............

You will need some paper.
Say to your child, 'We are going to draw a number.'
On a piece of paper draw a number 1. Make it large.
Say, 'This is number one.' Encourage your child to run
their finger over the number and say 'one'.

Draw the number in the air and encourage your child to
do the same.

Then on a piece of paper draw a number 2. Make it
large. Say, 'This is number two.' Encourage your child to
run their finger over the number and say 'two'.

Draw the number 2 in the air and encourage your child
to do the same.

During the week play this game as much as you can.

Date	☺ Comment

Number shapes

Ideas for Home

Play the number game

Date:............

Say to your child, 'We're going to play another number game. I am going to draw a number in the air and you have to see if you can remember its name.'

Draw a big **2**. See if they can guess 'two'. Encourage them to say 'two'.

Then draw **1**. See if they can guess 'one'.

If they find this difficult, keep playing with these two numbers.
If they can name the numbers, see if they can recognise them if you draw the number with your finger on their back.

Continue playing this game as much as you can during the week.

Date	☺ Comment

Diagonal

Ideas for Home

Play the diagonals game

Session 34: Introducing the word <u>diagonal</u>

Date:............

Draw a large square or cut out a square shape and explain to your child that, if you draw a line from corner to corner, it is called 'a diagonal'. Let your child practise doing this and telling you that it is a diagonal.

Find a square or oblong shape in the house or outside (a carpet, rug, lawn, or paving slab) and holding hands say, 'We are going to walk in a diagonal across this carpet/slab/lawn – from corner to corner.'

Play this game several times. See if your child can walk in a diagonal by himself or herself. On a warm day, give your child a brush and a bucket of water and let them practise drawing diagonals across the slabs in the garden.

Date	☺ Comment

Sideways

Ideas for Home

Play walking sideways

Session 35: Introducing the word <u>sideways</u>

Date:...........

Stand holding hands with your child in the garden or in a room at home.

Say, 'We are going to play a game – you do as I do.' Walk sideways across the room or garden with your child and say, 'We are walking **sideways** across the room.'

Then turn around at the corner and walk sideways again until you have moved all around the room or garden.

Now see if your child can make sideways steps by himself or herself. Say, 'Take one big sideways step. Take two small sideways steps,' etc.

Play this game several times, taking it in turns to give instructions to each other.

Date	☺ Comment

Forwards, backwards

Ideas for Home

Play the forwards, backwards, sideways, and the diagonal game

Session 36: Understanding the words <u>forwards</u>, <u>backwards</u>, <u>sideways</u> and <u>diagonal</u>

Date:...........

Hold hands with your child and say, 'We can walk forwards (and walk forwards together), backwards (and walk backwards together), sideways (walk sideways) and in a diagonal from corner to corner (walk diagonally together).'

Say to your child, 'I'm going to ask you to do some things and you have to listen very carefully.' Then ask your child to do things such as, 'Walk sideways two steps,' 'Walk forwards...stop,' 'Walk backwards three steps...stop,' etc.

This can be played with other children or adults, in the house, garden or park.

Have fun and enjoy.

Date	☺ Comment

Record Sheet

Session 1   Play the first and last game

Session 2   Find things that are the same

Session 3   Play the shape hunt game

Session 4   Continue the shape hunt game

Session 5   Play another shape game

Session 6   Play the triangle game

Session 7   Play the number 2 game

Session 8   Play the heavy and light game

Session 9   Play the clapping game

Session 10 More clapping games

Session 11 Play the long and short game

Session 12 Play more shape games

Record Sheet

Session 13 Play the heaviest bag game

Session 14 Play the lighest bag game

Session 15 Play the find the longest
string game

Session 16 Play find the shortest string

Session 17 Explore what a cube is

Session 18 Make a semicircle

Session 19 Make a cube

Session 20 Play the apples in the box

Session 21 Make a cylinder

Session 22 Play the shapes game

Session 23 Play hiding the shapes

Session 24 Make a time wheel

Record Sheet

Session 25 Play the time game

Session 26 More talking time games

Session 27 Play the adding game

Session 28 Play the taking away game

Session 29 Play the forwards and
backwards game

Session 30 More forwards and
backwards games

Session 31 Play the counting in twos game

Session 32 Play drawing numbers

Session 33 Play the number game

Session 34 Play the diagonals game

Session 35 Play walking sideways

Session 36 Play the forwards, backwards,
sideways game

Number Songs and Rhymes

Five Fat Sausages Sizzling in a Pan

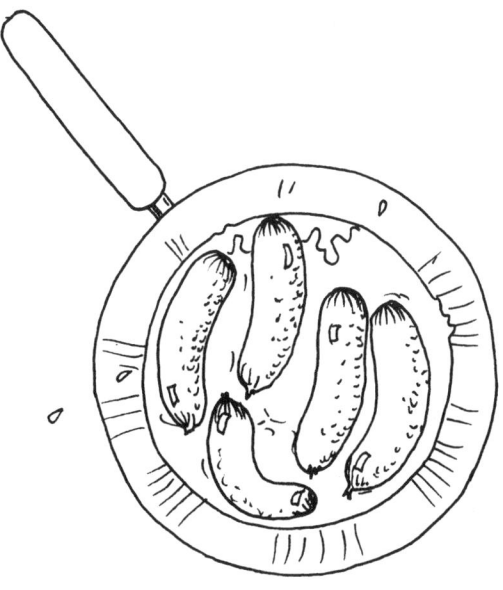

Five fat sausages sizzling in a pan,

All of a sudden one went bang.

There were four fat sausages sizzling in a pan,

All of a sudden one went bang.

There were three fat sausages sizzling in a pan,

All of a sudden one went bang.

There were two fat sausages sizzling in a pan,

All of a sudden one went bang.

There was one fat sausage sizzling in a pan,

All of a sudden one went bang.

There were no fat sausages sizzling in the pan.

There were Ten in the Bed

There were ten in the bed and the little one said,
'Roll over, roll over,'
So they all rolled over and one fell out.

10

There were nine in the bed and the little one said,
'Roll over, roll over,'
So they all rolled over and one fell out.

9

There were eight in the bed and the little one said,
'Roll over, roll over,'
So they all rolled over and one fell out.

8

There were seven in the bed and the little one said,
'Roll over, roll over,'
So they all rolled over and one fell out.

7

There were six in the bed and the little one said,
'Roll over, roll over,'
So they all rolled over and one fell out.

6

There were five in the bed and the little one said,
'Roll over, roll over,'
So they all rolled over and one fell out.

5

There were four in the bed and the little one said,
'Roll over, roll over,'
So they all rolled over and one fell out.

4

There were three in the bed and the little one said,
'Roll over, roll over,'
So they all rolled over and one fell out.

3

There were two in the bed and the little one said,
'Roll over, roll over,'
So they all rolled over and one fell out.

2

There was one in the bed and the little one said,
'Roll over, roll over,'
So they all rolled over and the little one fell out.

1

There were none in the bed and the little one said,
'Let's get back in bed now!'

0

Five Currant Buns in the Baker's Shop

Five currant buns in the baker's shop,
Round and fat with a currant on the top.
(Name of your child) came along to the
shop one day,
bought a currant bun and ate it
straight away.

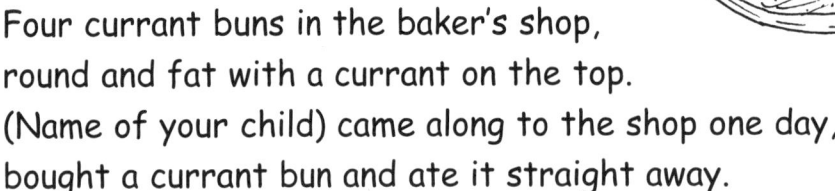

5

Four currant buns in the baker's shop,
round and fat with a currant on the top.
(Name of your child) came along to the shop one day,
bought a currant bun and ate it straight away.

4

Three currant buns in the baker's shop,
round and fat with a currant on the top.
(Name of your child) came along to the shop one day,
bought a currant bun and ate it straight away.

3

Two currant buns in the baker's shop,
round and fat with a currant on the top.
(Name of your child) came along to the shop one day,
bought a currant bun and ate it straight away.

2

One currant bun in the baker's shop,
round and fat with a currant on the top.
(Name of your child) came along to the shop one day,
bought a currant bun and ate it straight away.

1

There were no currant buns in the baker's shop,
round and fat with a currant on the top.
(Name of your child) came along to the shop one day,
There was no currant bun to eat and take away.

0

Five Little Monkeys Sitting in the Tree

Five little monkeys sitting in the tree,
Teasing Mr Crocodile, 'You can't catch me.'
Munch munch ching ching ching.

5

Four little monkeys sitting in the tree,
Teasing Mr Crocodile, 'You can't catch me.'
Munch munch ching ching ching.

4

Three little monkeys sitting in the tree,
Teasing Mr Crocodile, 'You can't catch me.'
Munch munch ching ching ching.

3

Two little monkeys sitting in the tree,
Teasing Mr Crocodile, 'You can't catch me.'
Munch munch ching ching ching.

2

One little monkey sitting in the tree,
Teasing Mr Crocodile, 'You can't catch me.'
Munch munch ching ching ching.

1

No little monkeys sitting in the tree,
Just one big fat crocodile you can see.
Munch munch ching ching ching.

0

Ten Little Bottles Standing in a Row

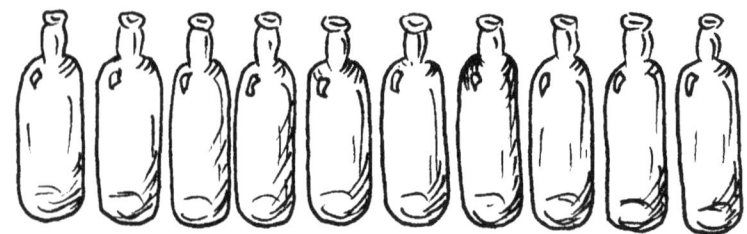

Ten little bottles standing in a row,
Ten little bottles standing in a row,
And if one little bottle should accidentally fall
There'd be **nine** little bottles standing in a row.

10

Nine little bottles standing in a row,
Nine little bottles standing in a row,
And if one little bottle should accidentally fall
There'd be **eight** little bottles standing in a row.

9

Eight little bottles standing in a row,
Eight little bottles standing in a row,
And if one little bottle should accidentally fall
There'd be **seven** little bottles standing in a row.

8

Seven little bottles standing in a row,
Seven little bottles standing in a row,
And if one little bottle should accidentally fall
There'd be **six** little bottles standing in a row.

7

Six little bottles standing in a row,
Six little bottles standing in a row,
And if one little bottle should accidentally fall
There'd be **five** little bottles standing in a row.

6

Five little bottles standing in a row,
Five little bottles standing in a row,
And if one little bottle should accidentally fall
There'd be **four** little bottles standing in a row.

5

Four little bottles standing in a row,
Four little bottles standing in a row,
And if one little bottle should accidentally fall
There'd be **three** little bottles standing in a row.

4

Three little bottles standing in a row,
Three little bottles standing in a row,
And if one little bottle should accidentally fall
There'd be **two** little bottles standing in a row.

3

Two little bottles standing in a row,
Two little bottles standing in a row,
And if one little bottle should accidentally fall
There'd be **one** little bottle standing in a row.

2

One little bottle standing in a row,
One little bottle standing in a row,
And if one little bottle should accidentally fall
There'd be **no** little bottles standing in a row.

1

0

81

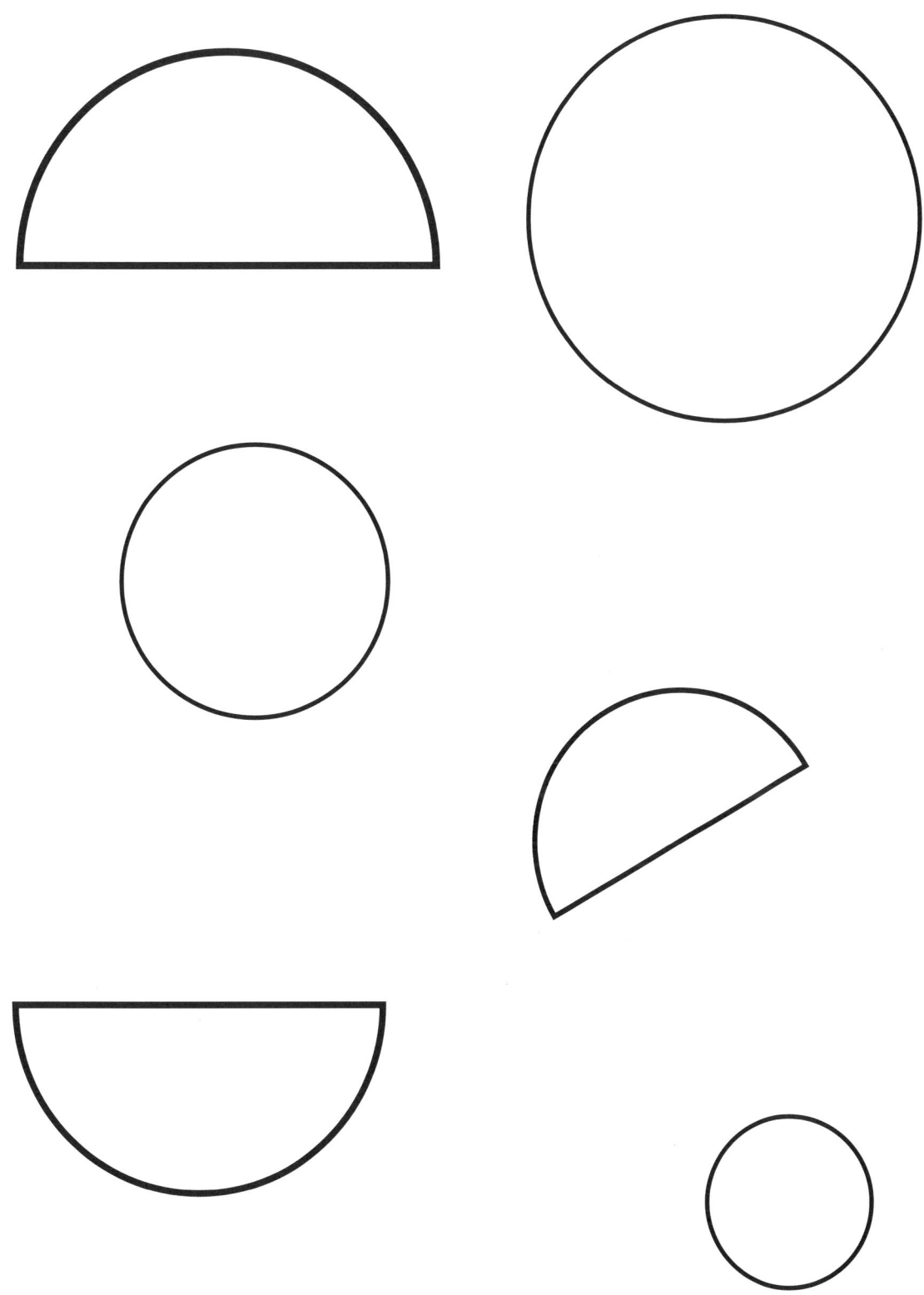

English

Language Development
Circle Time Sessions
to Improve Communication
Skills
£17.00 • 144pp
1-84312-156-5 • 2003

OUT NOW!

Language Development
Activities for Home
£12.00 • 144pp
1-84312-170-0 • January 2004

Maths

**Language Development
for Maths**
Circle Time Sessions to Improve
Language Skills
£18.00 • 144pp
1-84312-171-9 • August 2004

Aug 2004!

**Language Development
for Maths**
Activities for Home
£12.00 • 144pp
1-84312-172-7 • August 2004

Science

**Language Development
for Science**
Circle Time Sessions to Improve
Language Skills
£18.00 • 144pp
1-84312-173-5 • March 2005

March 2005

**Language Development
for Science**
Activities for Home
£12.00 • 144 pp
1-84312-174-3 • March 2005

Sample activities for school

KS2 Session 16

MATERIALS NEEDED
• Parrot, or ball.
• Cards showing pictures of mouse, hedgehog and butterfly.
• Picture/model of a dragon (see Appendix). Enlarge to A3 at least and colour and laminate.
• Feely bag with rhyming objects: 'at/in'.

Round
(Sitting)
1 With a responsive toy, e.g. a parrot, the child says his or her name and waits for a response.
Or
2 Roll the ball (saying 'I feel happy when . . .') then roll the ball to someone else.

Syllabilisation

mouse   hedgehog   butterfly

Lay out three cards, one with one syllable, one with two syllables, one with three syllables. Ponder about how many syllables/claps each has. An adult claps out the syllables, e.g.
hedge hog
clap   clap
The children have to guess which card you are thinking of after several turns. Change the cards.

Fruit in the fridge

Stage 1
Play one round of 'fruit box', where each child is identified with a fruit. Then play 'Sit down apples. Sit down pears. Stand up apples. Sit down bananas' and so on. (Check that all the children know which fruit they represent.)

77

...ar's Question Cards

Does it have wheels?	Where is it kept at night?
Does it travel along the ground?	Does it have an engine?
How many people can it hold?	

© 2002 Marion Nash et al. Language Development. ISBN 1 85346 879 7. P4...

Sample activities for home

IDEAS FOR HOME

Play the hiding under game

Early Years
Date:

Session One: Understanding the word 'under'

Get your child's duvet or sheet, put it on the floor and ask them to go UNDER it.

Say 'You are under the Duvet'. Take a turn yourself to sit under the duvet / sheet. Say 'I'm under too'.

Use the word 'under' and show your child things under as much as you can this week

Please complete delivery details

Name: ....

Organisation: ....

....

Address: ....

....

....

....

Postcode: ....

Tel: ....

ORDER FORM

Qty	ISBN	Title	Price	Subtotal
	1-84312-156-5	Language Development	£17.00	
	1-84312-170-0	Language Development	£12.00	
	1-84312-171-9	Language Development for Maths	£18.00	
	1-84312-172-7	Language Development Maths	£12.00	
	1-84312-173-5	Language Development for Science	£18.00	
	1-84312-174-3	Language Development Science	£12.00	
			P&P	
			TOTAL	

Free p&p for Schools, LEAs and other Organisations.

Payment

☐ Please invoice
(applicable to schools, LEAs and other institutions)
Invoices will be sent from our distributor, HarperCollins Publishers

☐ I enclose a cheque payable to David Fulton Publishers Ltd
(include postage and packing)

☐ Please charge to my credit card (Visa/MasterCard, American Express, Switch, Delta)

card number ☐☐☐☐☐☐☐☐☐☐☐☐☐☐☐☐☐☐☐

expiry date ☐☐☐☐

(Switch customers only) valid from ☐☐☐☐   issue number ☐

To order

Send to:
David Fulton Publishers, The Chiswick Centre, 414 Chiswick High Road, London W4 5TF

Freephone: **Fax:**
0500 618 052   020 8996 3622